"A poet is a historian. If they are tuned in to the community around them, their words can be important documents of an era. South Carolina is a complicated and beautiful place. If you want to know the nuance of the Palmetto State, read Marjory's poems."

MARCUS AMAKER,

Inaugural Poet Laureate of Charleston; Inductee, SC Literary Hall of Fame

Praise for

ONE RIVER, ONE BOAT

"I applaud Ms. Wentworth for her touching words and hope the people of South Carolina, across the country, and peoples around the world are as touched by her words as I have been."

CONGRESSMAN JAMES E. CLYBURN,
6th District of South Carolina, Congressional Record, January 14, 2015

"Although Marjory Wentworth was not born in South Carolina, this beautiful book's deep attachment to the state shines through in every line and sentence. The book is at once intensely personal and appropriately public, linking Wentworth's family history—the joys and anxieties of raising children – to the deeper, wider history of our state with all its beauty and violence. The scents, sounds and sights of Lowcountry South Carolina leap off the page as Wentworth tackles the "fault lines of our own making"—slavery, racial violence, political shenanigans—and examines our responses to natural disasters—earthquake, hurricanes, and the COVID pandemic. The poems and memoirs collected here jointly serve as a concise autobiography and history, all couched in Wentworth's crystalline, accessible language."

SIMON LEWIS,
Editor, *Illuminations, An International Magazine of Contemporary Writing*; Professor of English, The College of Charleston

"Water flowing, wings in flight, light illuminating the darkness. Marjory Wentworth is a poet of place, but her expansive imagination is ever asking us to think beyond the place and time—at times the darkness—in which we find ourselves. Wentworth describes Charleston as "a shrine to the past," and over and over she captures how time and history get confused in a city like Charleston and a state like South Carolina, so bound to the past. As she writes in the stunning title poem, "One River, One Boat," written for then-Governor Nikki Haley's second inauguration, "our history is a knot / we try to unravel, while others / try to tighten it." The poem addressed the difficulties of history—migrant workers, enslaved Africans, and the 2014 exoneration of a young black man wrongly convicted of murder in 1944—in order to emphasize the ties that bind us and the stakes of belonging. The powers that be dropped the poem from the state ceremony, just as a Civil War reenactment in another poem avoids the section of the city where enslaved Africans were sold—reminding us that every act of commemoration is also potentially an act of erasure. Wentworth's poetry documents and illuminates pivotal moments from her 17 years as the state's poet laureate—hurricanes, festivals, inaugurations and graduations, gifts and ghosts, and of course the horrific shooting at Mother Emanuel Church in 2015. History here may be distorted, but it may also be reimagined, restored. I linger over the poem Wentworth wrote in 2011 for students graduating from the Art Institute of Charleston (now gone, closed in 2018): "Take time to hover at the still / mouth of this ancient harbor / then rise into the air, which holds // a place for you." Rise into the air. This is a book of flight and transformation, of stillness and light. Yes, there is a place for you here."

ED MADDEN,

Author, *A Pooka in Arkansas* and *A Story of the City*; Poet Laureate, City of Columbia, SC (2015-2022)

BOOKS BY MARJORY WENTWORTH

Poetry:

Noticing Eden

Despite Gravity

The Endless Repetition of an Ordinary Miracle

New and Selected Poems

What the Water Gives Me

Prose:

Taking a Stand, The Evolution of Human Rights (co-writer)

We Are Charleston, Tragedy and Triumph at Mother Emanuel (co-writer)

Seeking, Poetry and Prose Inspired by the Art of Jonathan Green (co-editor)

Childrens:

Shackles

Out of Wonder, Poems Celebrating Poets (co-writer)

ONE RIVER, ONE BOAT

Occasional Poems and Other Stories

MARJORY WENTWORTH

South Carolina Poet Laureate 2003-2020

EVENING POST BOOKS

Published by
Evening Post Books
Charleston, South Carolina
www.eveningpostbooks.com

First edition.

Author: Marjory Wentworth
Editor: Elizabeth Hollerith and Jacob Hollifield
Cover and Layout design: Wesley Strickland

Front Cover: *Ashley River (SC).* Batik on Silk 67x35". Courtesy of Mary Edna Fraser.

First printing 2024.
Printed in the United States of America.

A CIP catalog record for this book has been applied for from the Library of Congress.

ISBN: 978-1-929647-99-6 (Paperback)

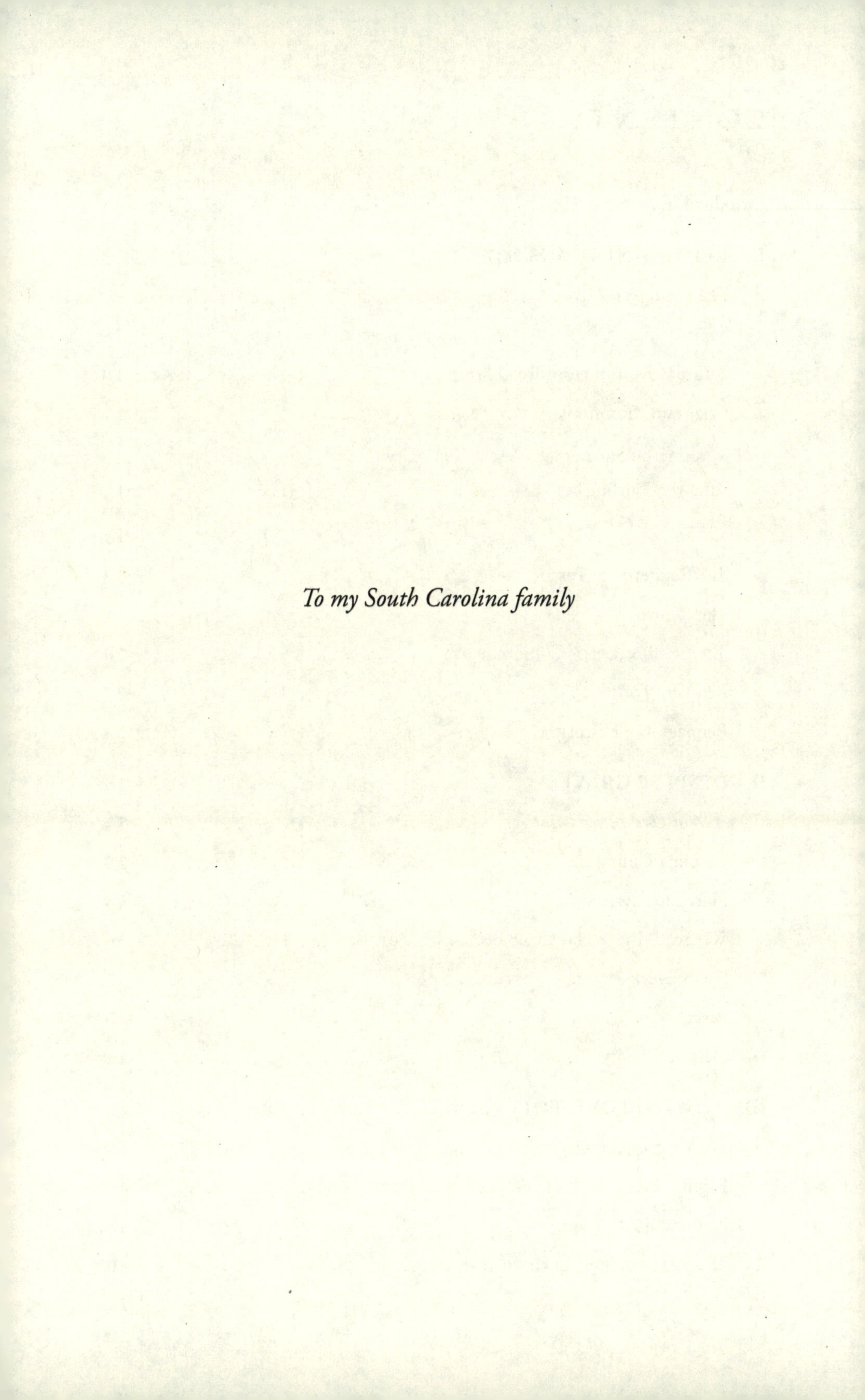

To my South Carolina family

CONTENTS

INTRODUCTION

Poets are often called upon to write something for an occasion, like a birthday or wedding celebration or, sadly, for a funeral. At moments of intense emotion, people crave language that articulates what they are feeling, which is often overwhelmed. This is why poetry books are often largely comprised of either love poems or eulogies.

Poets are essentially the translators of human emotion, because poems can condense and crystallize pain or express unfathomable joy. They acknowledge the worst of human behavior, while reminding us of the best things about being alive.

I am no exception. I started writing in middle school when my father was diagnosed with leukemia; the act of writing comforted me in a way that nothing else could. I literally stumbled onto writing verse, and the initial satisfaction of finding words that reflected my emotions stayed with me and determined the course of my life. There's really nothing quite like it.

I still have the red journal where I wrote my first poems. I didn't share them immediately, but I never stopped writing. Writing in private has a healing quality, but when the work is shared with others, there is an intense connection that transcends understanding. Through empathy, precise language, and imagery, poets connect us to the world and to one another.

I am grateful for the opportunity to share some of the works I wrote for countless occasions during my seventeen-year tenure as poet laureate of South Carolina.

— Marjory Wentworth

I. REIMAGINING HISTORY

"O how history intersects—"

— Natasha Tretheway

THE OCCASIONAL POEM

THE OCCASIONAL POEM IS WRITTEN FOR A PARTICULAR event. Often recited in public, when the audience listens but cannot read the lines, these poems need to work off the page and one must approach the writing with that in mind. Repetition is important, as well as precise imagery so listeners can more easily visualize the landscape or objects the writer describes. Usually there are no other poems recited at the event, which can work for or against the poet. Sometimes there is simply too much going on for people to really absorb the piece, and the words get lost in the shuffle. Often, the poem goes at the end of the event, when half the audience has already left and those that remain are getting antsy to leave. This is not ideal, believe me. Perhaps a plane flies overhead or a fire alarm goes off mid-poem. The possibilities are endless.

But there are also times when the poem is the placeholder for stillness and peace. It's the one moment for the audience to process the day and consider its unexpressed deeper meanings. And when this happens, it is magic. It's a trance that lasts for the duration of the recitation. The crowd is right there with you, and the connection between the poet and the audience is intense. You can hear a pin drop.

Much of the situation is out of your control, even at a highly organized event. At Governor Nikki Haley's inauguration in 2011, for example, a uniformed state trooper fainted and dropped like a rock — straight down on the cement steps very close to where I was sitting. He was revived and cared for by paramedics on-hand, but it was a frightening thing to watch.

The very first time I delivered an occasional poem was at Governor Mark Sanford's first inauguration; that too, was a frightening experience. I was seated beside Reverend Joseph Darby, who was the director of the NAACP at the time. His task was to lead us in an opening prayer, but Reverend Darby is African American, and white supremacists had made threats on his life. SLED sharpshooters were placed on top of the tall buildings surrounding the Statehouse. Everywhere I looked I could see them, with their weapons seemingly pointed right at us. I kept glancing at Reverend Darby, he was calm and collected. I am sure this was not the first time his life had been threatened by racists, nor would be his last. We have been friends ever since that day.

Sometimes the occasion is intensely emotional, and you are not sure you can make it through the poem without bursting into tears. Dottie Frank was one of my best friends, and her daughter Victoria asked me to read my poem "River" at her mother's funeral in 2019 at Charleston's Grace Church. I said yes, of course. But I was grieving deeply, and I barely made it through the thirty-six-lines of text.

Nothing was more difficult, however than drafting a poem in the dark days following the massacre at Charleston's Mother Emanuel AME Church in the summer of 2015. Everything I had learned and everything I believed about the power of verse became manifest in the eight short stanzas that comprise "Holy City."

At 9:05 p.m. on Wednesday, June 17th, nine people were murdered at the end of Bible study at Mother Emanuel AME Church. I knew some of the names printed in the newspaper the next morning; I had been to services and community events in this historic church. As poet laureate, I had programmed numerous events with librarian Cynthia Graham Hurd. In fact, Mother Emanuel is next door to the Main Library. My heart was broken, and I had no language to express this grief. But less than one day later, on Thursday evening as I was checking in seniors for graduation at The Art Institute of Charleston, Adam Parker called from *The Post and Courier* newspaper and asked me to write a poem for Sunday's paper. It would be included in a special pull-out section because the church would be open for services that Sunday. (The murders took place in the "church basement" below the sanctuary, so it remained unharmed.) The editors wanted to create something lasting, something people could keep. I considered what was required– a prayer of sorts, some words to help everyone process the horror.

The core of poetry's power is its ability to find language that describes the indescribable. And what we felt in Charleston in 2015 was overwhelming and incomprehensible. In the few hours that I had to write "Holy City," I read from the great post-World War II Polish poets Czeslaw Milosz and Wislawa Szymborska. The poems that had grown out of the violence they had witnessed in their homeland spoke to me across the decades. I thought about Reverend Pinckney, who was the minister at Mother Emanuel, and what a great orator he was. Thanks to my friend Mary Edna Fraser, I found a talk that he had done online during which he said what we all needed to hear: "Only Love Can Conquer Hate." I wrote that down, and then the poem came. And though I have read the poem on multiple occasions, I will never be able to share it without choking back tears.

On discovering that Sullivan's Island was the place where approximately 40,000 captured Africans were quarantined after enduring the Middle Passage.

SAND

"The eye is not satisfied with seeing, not the ear with hearing."
— Ecclesiastes

Each day I awaken in darkness,
to the joy of that particular silence
when the earth becomes herself again
shedding centuries of clutter. Even here
the fort and cannons disappear. Every building
is erased by night. Only the moon and stars
remain and the waves rolling over sand
sounding like steady distant breaths.

Your breath is everywhere, dissolving like hours.
Only now can you enter my heart.
It is a small, crowded place -
like this island, once a brief cluster
of weeds and sand, now filling
with high houses built one on top
of the other. Each one bigger than the last,
assuming a kind of permanence.

You have watched it all come and go.
Conquerors, pirates, soldiers, and slaves.
Long battles at sea. The violence
that began a nation, and later divided it.
Consider the soldiers who washed up
like dead fish, or the countless Africans

who came ashore in chains and never left
the *lazaretto.* Buried in mass graves
unmarked and unvisited, they remain
and outnumber all who have followed.

Day after day the wind sweeps across the island
smothering the shattered bones and blood
in layers of swirling sand. I gather handfuls
and watch it scatter through my fingers.
This is all that remains
beneath seaweed, stars, and sweet myrtle;
sea birds scattered in the rain.

I lower my head and remember
this is where you live and suffer.
In the stillness, I see the things that are
not visible. I hear voices
no one else can hear, except for you.

On the occasion of a spring day in downtown Charleston at The Confederate Home, originally known as the Home for the Mothers, Widows, and Daughters of Confederate Soldiers.

SATURDAY MORNING ON BROAD STREET

Where flowers are never forgotten
behind walls of stone and all that has
gathered   coins and smoke
church bells like wind   just here
beneath a cloud clotted sky   the scent
of last night's rain   ladies
wearing cotton blouses   doing laundry
in the little white room downstairs
they say the funniest things   later
a wedding out on the lawn   voices at dusk
violins   tea olives   a cardinal
brightening the fig tree   my heart
lives here   not really.

Capt. Richard G. Cliff Jr., 29, of Mount Pleasant, South Carolina, was killed in Yakhchal, Afghanistan, September 29, 2008.

CHARLESTON ROOFTOPS

Everything that lifts into the air
has purpose: even the granite tipped war
monument rising above palmetto trees
points like an arrow toward the sun;
chimneys, stove pipes, weathervanes, and steeples -
the flag at half mast, flapping in the wind.

Streets clog with memories of smoke-tinged wind –
of a dark sky on fire fueling the air,
flames swirling around steeples,
and a harbor blocked by ships of war.
Cannons fired toward the ever-present sun
until the avenues lined with oak trees

were abandoned, and the trees
thrust transcendent into the wind
reached like prayers toward the sun.
Odors of ruin and rot lingered in the air
above the streets emptied by war;
the bells silent in the steeples.

Beyond scaffold enshrouded steeples,
sunlight weaves through leaf-thick oak trees
now filled with blossom and song, though war
saturates the brick and memory of wind
spinning with salt through summer air
that simmers beneath the blood-streaked sun.

Red runs through ribbons of sun
across the skyline and steeples
lifting off tin sloped roofs into air
filled with flowering trees.
Always the tireless ocean wind
ripples the worn-out flags of war.

The names of the enemy change, but war
is the inscrutable language spoken beneath this sun.
The flag at half-mast stiffens in the wind.
Funeral bells sound from the steeples.
In the cemetery, beneath the oak trees,
taps linger on the broken air.

The sounds of war will rumble in the wind.
As steeple bells call through the sun filled air,
birds nest in trees twisting toward heaven.

The largest recorded earthquake in the history of the southeastern United States occurred near Charleston, South Carolina, August 31, 1886.

WASHINGTON SQUARE, CHARLESTON TENT CITY AFTER THE EARTHQUAKE 1886

I no longer count the days
nor the long-scorched nights passing
like lifetimes. As soon as sleep
finds me, I am running alone
through the dark, while walls crumble
and the earth rumbling low
like a wounded animal,
rises and pitches beneath me.

If not for the chimney bricks
falling fast from the sky
I would swear I was at sea,
like a small boat in a storm.
And this is how I feel
when I wake in the damp tent-
my husband snoring beside me,
the child inside my belly
flipping like a confused fish.

I light a candle and walk
outside. The moon hanging low
brightens the September sky,
and I almost believe what they say
about the world not ending.
I count the stars as if they are
my blessings, tiptoe back inside,

and touch the things we salvaged
stacked on a table: my brush
and comb, one silver candlestick,
the family Bible missing
its heavy brown cover.

For The Poetics of Witness program, the Gibbes Museum of Art, September 20, 2023.

1937

I never imagined my grandmother at rest,
until I saw the Dorothea Lange photograph
of a *sharecropper wife and mother of seven*
children near Chesenee, South Carolina;
because this woman is so relaxed,
as if her endless work is done.
Sitting on a chair – one arm stretched across
her swollen belly, the other hand
holding her chin; deep in thought,
her eyes are focused on something outside
the frame, dreaming into the distance,
she looks as if she can see beyond
the cotton fields and the small town
where she was born,
before the babies came one after the other,
before the lean years, when the store
still had barrels full of flour,
oats, and rows of sugary canned fruit
lining the dusty shelves.
After the war to end all wars,
she was young, and life was sweet,
the way it must have seemed
to my grandmother, before giving
birth to eight children on the kitchen table
in the gabled house on a bog road
across the stand of apple trees
in West Bethel, Maine, where snowdrifts

reached the roof most winters,
and mud clogged the roads each spring.

In Hebrew, Bethel means house of God.
Sometimes, she must have wondered
where God was in that house west of Bethel,
those grueling years of war and rationing,
when the babies came one after the other.
My mother, number 5, was the fattest.
After three boys in a row, she was adored –
the only one to find a tangerine in the toe
of her Christmas stocking, beneath peppermints
and a pair of red mittens knit by her mother.
She had never seen a tangerine,
and did not know how to eat it. At first,
she thought it was a ball that she could roll
across the floor and watch the black barn cat
try to catch it. This story was her easy way
of explaining how poor they were,
and how my grandmother could make a holiday
out of almost nothing. Like the mother
in the photograph in Chesnee, South Carolina,
who sat down at the end of the long day,
watched the sun setting over the peach trees,
this woman who believed that the pink light
spreading across the tops of the flowering
branches were shining just for her.

On seeing a photograph taken by Lauren Preller-Chambers.

THE REINTERMENT PARADE

Charleston, South Carolina 1999

If it weren't for the parked cars and sunburned tourists lining the cracked sidewalks, you might guess a Civil War movie was being filmed on this cobblestone street. Iron black crosses pressed into gray stone walls straighten the earthquake-bent foundations. Beneath flickering gaslights, houses with sagging porches that face the sea lean toward each other as if time has blended wood and paint and glass into a permanent wound.

The Confederate Carriage Company carries coffins covered in mourning ribbons. Women dressed as *widows* walk silently behind, wearing short black veils, capes, and hoop skirts. They do not turn toward the crowd as they follow a soldier high on a horse, carrying a new Confederate Battle flag. Marching toward the graveyard now, there is nowhere else to go. Some of them carry damp white handkerchiefs in their gloved hands. Some clutch a family Bible. Others hold photographs lined with crushed crimson velvet. They are grim-faced and stoic, a little proud. Their great, great grandmothers might have lived through the war. Women who lived so long in terror that they always expected the worst. Women who were sure, Sherman would burn Charleston to the ground, and steal everything, everything. They dressed in layers, with two petticoats hiding beneath their dresses, and jewelry sewn into the layer closest to their skin. They were women who had lost their husbands and their fathers, their brothers, and their uncles. In the end, all they had was one another.

The re-enactors march away from the sea. Beyond the seawall lies the harbor where the sailing ships brought Africans in chains. A few streets inland is the market where the captured Africans were sold; the parade will not pass by there.

On the occasion of Michael B. Moore's campaign launch for US Congress in South Carolina's 1st District, March 2024.

THE RETURN

For Michael B. Moore

"My race needs no special defense, for the past history of them in this country proves them to be the equal of anyone anywhere. All they need is the equal chance in the battle of life."
— Robert Smalls

Where the sea wanders, spilling
Through salt marsh awash
In sunrise and gull chatter,
A Great Egret tiptoes
Across mud flats, watching
The silver flash of fish
Leaping toward a dream.

This is the place you chose-
Where water is a witness,
Washing away wounds
Long buried by the sweep
Of distorted history
And the glory of this landscape
Shaped by the inescapable
Movement of the sea.

You returned to this storm
Battered coast where your destiny
Was written before you were born,
To build a sacred space,
Out of suffering and hope
Rising above Gadsden's Wharf.

And you stayed, as the winds
Swirled and the tides rose
And fell around you,
Because you believed
In making something better.

We praise your courage
To enter the fray and lead.
And we will follow,
Because you are the one,
your ancestors dreamed of.

For the opening of Flight, a visual arts exhibit featuring the work of artist Mary Edna Fraser, Aiken-Rhett House, Charleston, South Carolina, November 2022.

THE ARCHITECTURE OF CONTAINMENT

Enslaved Quarters Part 1

In the small square bedroom
above the kitchen, heat rose
from the stove in waves so heavy
it was almost visible. A family
trying to sleep here, would lie still
as long as possible, tossing
and turning beneath moonlight, pouring
through the only open window.

Sometimes a breeze
carrying the scent of the sea
rippled through the thick air
as if it could change everything.

But the window turned in
on itself, on them, and their entire world.

The city beyond the high walls
was as far away as the moon itself.

Even the horses, snorting
in the stables
across the courtyard
could sometimes see beyond these walls.

Flocks of seagulls would often
find their way here—strutting around the grounds
then rising through the line
of magnolias
high above the walls.
Some would hover, almost still—
suspended in the air like hope.

For The Requiem for Rice service, Mother Emanuel AME Church, Charleston, South Carolina, October 22, 2017.

REQUIEM FOR RICE

For Jonathan Green

When we walk from the sea
Along the river
Filling with tides,
We will bend down
To plant rice in mud
That was here before
We came. Water
Touching roots, growing
Beyond memory.

We will pass
Neglected
Graves
Of the enslaved.
The earth holds
Their names
The way it holds rain.

We will dig through
Centuries until
We find them,
Bent to earth
Bent to water
We will plant rice
Beyond the numbers
Beyond the names.

On the occasion of Mayor John Tecklenburg's inauguration, January 11, 2016.

REIMAGINING HISTORY

By Marcus Amaker and Marjory Wentworth

Though Charleston is a shrine to the past,
where every alleyway and weather-worn road
tells the story of a city resurrected;
time is never standing still.
Running beneath the surface
are fault lines of our own making,
reshaping memory brick by brick.

Hours crumble in the soil at Hampton Park,
where horses ran laps for sport,
and Union soldiers were laid to rest,
honored as "Martyrs of the Race Course."
Now, a statue of Denmark Vesey stands
in this place named for a confederate general,
as flowers bloom among the ruins.

This year, we've done laps around despair;
we've grown tired of running in circles
so we stepped off the track and began to walk.
As the earth shifts beneath our feet,
we move forward together. Our hearts
unhinged, guide us toward a city
remade by love, into a future
that our past could never have imagined,
beginning today.

II. DESPITE GRAVITY

"My wound is my geography."

— Pat Conroy

A MOST UNEXPECTED MUSE

THIS IS A STORY ABOUT A NATURAL DISASTER, A FLOODED home, and a displaced family; but it's also a story about resurrection from the ruins. It is, therefore, a quintessentially Southern story. It is the story of my family's life on Sullivan's Island—the place we raised our children with a freedom that few children still experience—where they rolled out of bed every morning, put on their backpacks, walked across the street past the Poe Library, and went to school with a view of the ocean. After school, they arrived home at a door facing the sea that was always open, because we never had a key. The island was their playground, from Stella Maris Church to the bamboo forest on the hill, from Breech Inlet to Officer's Row; and that's where our three little boys, hair bleached blond by the sun, played their hearts out every single day of their childhood. At Fort Moultrie, they could run through the tunnels to escape the British. On the backside of the island, they built a fort in the marsh grass. In our backyard they had a swing set and a sandbox, trees for climbing, and a garden bursting with cucumbers, okra, tomatoes, and watermelon. They spent long days at the beach, where they swam almost year-round, built sandcastles, caught crabs, went boogie boarding and surfed. Those days, rolling one on top of the other, are a continuous dream of childhood.

Like many people you meet in Charleston, we just landed here. We were looking to move out of our Brooklyn apartment when my husband Peter was offered a job with a film company based in Charleston. When we first moved to Sullivan's Island that summer of 1989, it was still a funky place filled with old, run-down beach houses that had been in families for generations, and it had a small-town feel that appealed to us after living in the city for a decade. In those days, there was no Isle of Palms connector, no 5,000-square-foot mansions, Mr. Gruber still ran "The Wishing Well," an old convenience store, and houses cost less than $200,000. Everyone seemed to know everyone else. We bought a run-down gatehouse on Middle Street with a huge backyard where our sons could play. It was built in 1853 and had survived hurricanes, earthquakes, and the Civil War. Although the air-conditioning was spotty, the windows wouldn't open, and there were leaks in the roof and only one closet, the house had a charm that suited us. The minute we walked through the front door, we were home.

Since the island is only a half-mile wide, the sense of the sea was palpable. Even though we could only see the ocean from the third floor "crow's nest," we could always smell the salt and hear the waves moving on shore. The lighthouse was only a couple of blocks away, and at night the great light would shine into our bedrooms as it made its never-ending circle. After a few nights, the light became a comforting presence.

I grew up in a small coastal town north of Boston, and I am used to being lulled to sleep by the sound of foghorns, but truth be told I had always felt an awkward sense of estrangement from my homeplace. Although both my family and my husband's family have lived in New England for centuries, I knew I belonged somewhere else. I just didn't know where that was. I could never have imagined it would be anyplace south of the Mason-Dixon Line, but so it goes.

In New England, the same metal-colored sky can last for months at a time, especially in early winter. On Sullivan's Island at sunset, the sky turned from yellow to pink a million different ways. The light falling upon the earth here must be like the light shining in heaven. The landscape was exotic, lush, and sensual. Palmetto and banana trees were scattered through the back yard that took up two lots. Trumpet vine climbed the fences. Everything was blooming in the thick humid air that summer before Hurricane Hugo. I was dazzled. I love New York, but the entire time I lived there I craved nature. Like many poets, I look to the natural world for meaning and metaphors.

We were still unpacking boxes and getting to know our neighbors when we had to evacuate for Hurricane Hugo that September. We had so little time to board up and pack the car that we didn't have a chance to find the box with our sons' birth certificates. We knew the hurricane was coming straight for us. Nothing would ever be the same for our family or this small island we had just started to call home.

Two days after Hurricane Hugo made landfall, we drove back from Columbia on Route 26, not knowing what we would find, if anything. Rumors were circulating that all the barrier islands were still covered in water. We were terrified. There were hardly any cars on the road. Things looked fairly normal until we got about thirty miles outside of Charleston. None of the traffic lights worked because there was no power. The entire forest on either side of the highway had been flattened by the high winds. Every single tree trunk was snapped in two. It looked like bombs had been dropped. We drove with the windows down, and the absence of sound was haunting. The hum of everyday life was missing in the air. Whenever we passed a clump of people waiting in line for water or food, the silence continued. It was as if people were too shocked to speak to one another. We just kept going.

The National Guard seemed to be everywhere in Charleston. We hitched a boat ride out to Sullivan's Island, since the Ben Sawyer Bridge was flipped open during the storm. When we got off the Boston Whaler near Station 24, we got a ride down Middle Street in one of their trucks. Since so many wires were down it was dangerous to walk anywhere. There were lots of people in the back of the truck. One woman was crying uncontrollably, another woman vomited over the side. The truck stopped about a quarter of a mile from our house because another house was in the middle of the road and there was no way to drive around it. We couldn't see beyond the wreckage. A man took my hand when we climbed out of the back and said, "May God be with you." Peter and I ran down the street, hurtling over tree trunks and garbage cans. Our eight- month-old son Oliver was in a backpack, and he thought this part was funny. And suddenly there was our house. Hallelujah. The live oak in the front yard hadn't crushed our roof. The yard was filled with smashed muddy furniture, someone's dishwasher, surfboards, and lawn chairs—just endless wet stuff tangled in the downed tree limbs. One block over, a tornado took out every single home in its path. We felt lucky.

Inside was another story. Every single thing was covered in wet mud and sand. Every piece of furniture, every dish, every spoon. The tidal surge had left two and half feet of mud on the first floor. The smell of mold and mildew was overwhelming. It would last for months. My husband's brothers flew down from Maine with their chainsaws. They did their best to clean up, but by the end of October electricity was sporadic at best.

We tried moving back home. Neighbors had left baby food and a box of diapers at our front door. We ate meals served by the Red Cross at the Baptist church down the road. Donations came in from all over the country. Our four-year-old son Hunter was overjoyed to find boxes of his favorite Kraft macaroni and cheese. The Red Cross lady gave him six boxes. Black marker messages were written in a child's scrawl across the blue and yellow cardboard. "From the children of Toledo, Ohio," one read. Another had a personal note: "I hope you like macaroni and cheese as much as I do." It was signed like a letter— "your friend, Amy." Another box that I saved said "we are praying for you in Alabama." Was this my life? Helicopters flew overhead. All day long the sound of chainsaws filled the air. It was beyond chaotic.

It wasn't safe to stay in our house on Middle Street. The ceilings were filled with water and the basic structure of the house was not sound. We settled into a condominium on the Isle of Palms that my friend Louisa found for us. There were sheets and towels and pots and pans, and the electricity and running water worked all the time. Finally, we could settle down and begin to rebuild our lives. That winter we hired a contractor to replace floors and walls and the thousands of other things that needed to be done to make our Sullivans Island home habitable. By spring, most of the debris was picked up along the roadside, both lanes of the Ben Sawyer Bridge were finally working, and everywhere you looked something was blooming. I had never seen such abundance—honeysuckle, wild roses, and Carolina jessamine crawling wild along every fence filling the air with scent.

After eight months, thanks to our neighbors, we were able to move back to Sullivan's Island to the little blue gingerbread house almost next door to our house, which was months away from completion. But finally, we were back home on the island where our newfound friends lived.

That summer after Hurricane Hugo, day-to-day life finally took on a kind of normalcy. I was pregnant with our third son Taylor, and I began to write poems again. I felt an intense connection with the landscape that I would not have had if we hadn't seen it virtually destroyed only months earlier. As construction began on our house, my belly grew, and the land itself seemed to be healing. The poems I wrote had an underlying emotional intensity. I never considered myself a landscape poet, but I clung to the imagery surrounding me on the island and I wrote my way out of the pain that characterized that year. Funny how life works, but the poems eventually formed a book called *Noticing Eden* and I began my life as a published poet.

Our attachment to Sullivan's Island, which is fierce and hard-earned, is hard to explain and still difficult to talk about because we no longer call this fragile barrier island our home. The roof leak was never really fixed, the walls were never completely dried out, and the endless problems with mold and termites just wore us down. When Hunter graduated from high school, we waved the white flag and moved to Mt. Pleasant to a home with heating and air-conditioning in every room. But for us and many others who lived through Hurricane Hugo, it will always be home. Sullivan's Island is a most unexpected muse, and despite everything I am eternally grateful.

Hurricane Hugo, a Category 4 storm, made landfall north of Charleston at Sullivan's Island, September 21-22, 1989.

CAROLINA UMBRA

Boats fly out of the Atlantic
and moor themselves in my backyard
where tiny flowers, forgotten
by the wind, toss their astral heads
from side to side. Mouths ablaze, open,
and filling with rain.

After the hurricane, you can see
the snapped open drawbridge slide
beneath the waves on the evening news.
You go cold imagining
such enormous fingers of wind
that split a steel hinge until
its jaw opens toward heaven.

Above the twisted house,
above this island, where the torn
churches have no roofs, and houses
move themselves around the streets
as if they were made of paper;
tangled high in the oak branches,
my son's crib quilt waves its pastel flag.

But the crib rail is rusted shut.
And you can't see my children
huddled together on the one dry bed
of this home filling with birds

that nest in corners of windowless rooms,
or insects breeding in the damp sand
smeared like paint over the swollen floors.

The storm will not roar in your sleep
tonight, as if the unconscious
articulations of an animal aware
of the end of its life were trapped
in the many cages of your brain.

You can't see grief darken the wind
rising over the islands. Tonight,
as the burning mountains of debris
illuminate the sky for hundreds of miles,
I see only the objects of my life
dissolving in a path of smoke.

All the lost and scattered hours
are falling completely out of time.
where endless rows of shredded trees wait
with the patience of unburied
skeletons, accumulating in the shadows.

On rebuilding after Hurricane Hugo and choosing to stay in South Carolina.

HURRICANE SEASON

The blood moon thirsts. All night,
listening to unspoken prayers,
she tugs the sea beyond itself
until redundant waves retreating
wash the yellowed marshes clean.

In the heat that follows too much rain,
people crowd the churches.
On this September Sunday morning
their hymns begin to rise
and slap the winds still raging.

This is the music of bones
entwined in mortal language -

words of those who know the wind
erases every footprint carved in earth
where water, tired as a dreamer,
circling beneath oblivious clouds
blurs the variations painted on each human face.

Into the open womb of the sea
descend the ashes of our sins.

What keeps us here? Not gravity
or light, but rust on fences, holding
every house of swollen wood, an ache
a tooth, the day moon adrift
grinding tiny islands down to bone.

For John Duckworth, Photography, 2011.

WHERE A MIRAGE HAS ONCE BEEN, LIFE MUST BE

in the blur of passing hours
accumulating as perfect circles
of light   green gold   odor
river   rising   mud washed
slipper strewn   tinged   with moonlight
paused   for one undulating kiss

after love   their long bodies
rise from the earth   marsh grass straightening
behind them   marking that patch of joy
already   darkening   they stumble
through ripe fields of abandoned
rice   rippling   in the wet wind

toward the sea   where waves shape
stones   into piles   marking the edge
stillness   water   ribboned
violet blue layers   of light
wrapping   unraveling
as permanent   as earth   imagined

or this day   stretching across dreams
like smoke   swirling beneath them   and within

For the novel, Shem Creek, By Dorothea Benton Frank, 2004.

SHEM CREEK

I.

The swollen earth splits its skin
into waterways, scattered
and winding in every
direction, releasing winds
that carve the land to shreds. Where
sun-filled clumps of spartina,
smoothed into supplicating
rows of heavy bent heads, crowd
the edges of Shem Creek;
marsh wrens build their tiny nests.
As if they are playing hide
and seek, dolphins appear
then disappear below the sea.
Fish birds littering the sky:
egrets, gray herons, and terns,
oyster catchers, pelicans,
gulls diving and turning through
the thick pink tinted air.

II.

Weaving through miles of treeless
Subdivisions and strip malls,
the creek gathers everything
from oil, soap, and gasoline
to tires and refrigerators.
After the rain, run-off fills

the oyster beds with dioxins.
Arsenic and mercury
drift through the water in clumps
of invisible clouds
as if no one will notice.

III.

Beyond the clutter of traffic,
tourist shops, seafood restaurants,
hotels, bars, and parking lots;
docked shrimp boats bob up and down
beside the docks, where the creek
pours silently into the sea.

After visiting the ACE Basin for the first time, the largest area of protected wetlands in North America.

RIVER

The river is a woman who is never idle.
Into her feathering water
fall petals and bones

of earth's shed skins.
While all around her edges
men are carving altars,

the river gathers flotsam,
branches of time, and clouds
loosening the robes of their reflections.

Her dress is decoupage -
yellow clustering leaves,
ashes, paper, tin, and dung.

Wine dark honey for the world,
sweet blood of seeping magma
pulsing above the carbon starred

sediment. Striped with settled skulls,
wing, and leaf spine: the river
is an open-minded graveyard.

Listen to the music
of sunlight spreading
inside her crystal cells.

Magnet, clock, cradle
for the wind, the river holds a cup
filling with miles of rain.

But when the river sleeps,
her celestial children
break the sticks of gravity,

grab fistfuls of fish
scented amber clotted with diamonds,
ferns, and petalling clouds,

adorn bracelets of woven rain,
rise with islands of sweet grass
and stars strung to their backs

to wander over the scarred surface
of the earth, like their mothers
simply searching for the sea.

For the opening and dedication ceremony of the Arthur Ravenel Jr. Bridge, Charleston, South Carolina, July 2005.

DESPITE GRAVITY

They come from France, Sweden, Mexico and Maine.
Designers and engineers cradling blueprints
and calculations in their arms; ironworkers
wearing hard hats and steel-toed boots, sledgehammers grasped
in the grip of their gloved hands. With scars and sweat
drying on their skin, they come with memories
of the sea and gorges sliced between mountains;
rivers with forgotten names moving beneath them,
time rushing overhead, and the knowledge of birds
flowing in their blood. On a boat before dawn
they cross the water. Starlight washes over them.
The air is moist and cool. And they are silent.
They are grateful for the silence. All day
it stays with them, as they work at the edge of the sky.

They come, because a bridge is like a dream
of what is possible. It rises from the earth
as if gravity was something imagined,
and the forces of the universe were suspended.
Workers take plywood and steel, construct a framework
into the endless air, where cables holding
a million pounds of iron and concrete
are as elegant as the strings on a harp
playing the sounds of wind rising off water.

In memory of Miguel Angel Rojas Lucas, who fell to his death during construction of the Arthur Ravenel Jr. Bridge

III. HOW TO LOVE THIS WORLD

"What is poetry that does not save
Nations or people?"
—Czeslaw Milosz

ILLUMINATING THE DARKNESS

Poetry and Empathy

"The precise role of the artist, then, is to illuminate that darkness, blaze roads through the vast forest, so that we will not, in all our doing, lose sight of its purpose, which is, after all, to make the world a more human dwelling place."

—"The Creative Process" by James Baldwin

THIS ESSAY BY JAMES BALDWIN IS A KIND OF CREDO FOR me, and it is the first reading assignment for most of the classes that I teach. The ideas in the essay are profound, but it's the poetic devices that elevate the text- consider the way he uses the image of blazing roads through the vast forest to amplify his statement about the creative process – one that illuminates the darkness. The sentence is full of figurative language.

I deeply believe that literature has the capacity to illuminate the world, rather than darken it. Creative people rely on their imaginations, and it often takes a great deal of imagination to envision a world that is different (more compassionate) than the one we inhabit. Artists and poets naturally question cultural norms and existing and accepted structures. Poet Adrienne Rich wrote – "The impulse to enter, with other humans, through language, into the order and disorder of the world, is poetic at its root..." So really it comes down to a kind of chosen engagement with the world, rather than running away in fear.

Poets connect us to the things of this world and to one another. Ultimately, poems articulate our shared humanity.

I have been fortunate to travel many places as poet laureate, from Bismarck, North Dakota to Mussoorie, India. What a glorious journey it has been.

FLIGHT

Clouds disassembling
Breathless in sunlight

Solid as the afternoon
I am not a part of

That is the place
I am looking for

The earth's magnet
Of troubles, spinning

As far away
As I am travelling

LEAP for Ghana Program, Summer 2014.

NOTHING IS ABANDONED

Lined with miles of tangled vines,
coconut palms and bananas
growing thick and green,

the dirt road to the market
climbs through clumps of tangerine
bougainvillea and trees

laden with lemons and limes,
passing pink painted box homes
where bright laundry is always

drying outside on the line,
and roosters pecking at the earth
announce the day triumphant.

The road is the color
of the sun rising over the sea.
There is smoke on the wind

and prayers playing on the radio,
as the road fills with people
walking in the same direction.

Everyone carries something:
buckets of picked peanuts,
a small child on her mother's back,

bags filled with mangoes, sugar cane
stacked on a tray. An endless
array of items passes by, from loaves

of bread to used batteries;
nothing goes to waste
in this roadside economy.

And nothing is abandoned
on this road pulsing with light
and the gifts the world brings.

For the graduating class of Mt. Holyoke College in South Hadley, Massachusetts that entered school in September 2001 and experienced 9/11, Spring 2005.

THE SOUND OF YOUR OWN VOICE SINGING

You came to this valley with expectations
you could not name but felt deeply, stumbling
out of the shadows of the twentieth century,
mumbling words that were distant but held you close
to the tortured world: Hiroshima, Auschwitz, My Lai.

Days felt like dreams. You remember
a house where music played through the night
and windows opened to the world. Rooms filled
with people you didn't know but recognized.
It was a place you felt safe. A house with no shadows.

How quickly death descended and shattered
that bright September Tuesday morning.
Down, down, down dropped the bodies
into the darkness and the sorrow
into the city smothered in paper and ash.

You came stumbling out of the smoke
into a room filling with sunlight and strangers.
You loved each one fiercely, as though they were your own,
and tenderness became the only way
to survive your time on earth.

The weight of love is the heaviest burden
you have learned to carry.
In the silence of the heavens,
it's a dream that wakes you
with the sound of your own voice singing.

In commemoration of the 70th Anniversary of the Closing of the International Military Tribunal at Nuremberg (1946), Nuremberg, Germany, October 2016.

IN THE SHADOWS OF NUREMBERG

For Henry Barbanel, Holocaust survivor and Nazi resistance fighter

Because we are forever weak
and wounded, looking for someone
to follow or blame; sometimes
we become savage and change
the rules to ease our minds.
Clouded by delusions
of power or fame, human
beings can justify anything.

Too often things can go wrong
in a hurry, and the masses
go along as if their hearts
were turned inside out, and hatred
was something long hidden
but there, like a riptide
pulling below the glittering
smooth surface of the sea.

Abandoning everything
we know is right, we become
tribal and primitive,
tearing the ties that bind us
one to another, as if
they were made of air. And love
dissolves into something
lost in the cruel cacophony.

And though it may be far,
there is always a storm
swirling somewhere. The sea
that connects and creates us,
holds the seeds of our destruction.
Still, God keeps nothing from us.
Each new wave is a renewal;
every day a gift of our own making.

As we stumble from the shadows
of the twentieth century,
covered in blood and ash,
cradling the bones of those who are lost,
we know there can be justice;
the pattern has been set.
No matter how long it takes,
there is no peace without redemption.
Without shadows, there is no light.

On reading that school bells were banned in Somalia, April 2012.

MILITANTS BAN SCHOOL BELLS IN A TOWN IN SOMALIA

Because school bells sound like church bells
and conflict with Islam, teachers slap the doors
when the class period is finished, which is confusing
for students and everyone is late for class.

Bras are banned for their western connotations.
So are soccer games, which have nothing to do
with women's undergarments. Even the mundane
aspects of daily life are controlled by strict edicts.

Music is outlawed in Mogadishu.
This ultimatum left broadcasters
scrambling to find creative ways
around the ban, leading them to play

recordings of horses galloping, roosters
crowing, engines roaring or guns being fired –
a common sound in the capital –
to signal the start of various broadcasts.

All internationally recognized holidays are banned,
but stoning and amputation of feet and hands
are on the rise among thieves. And fear, of course,
is palpable and intended. This is not news.

Alton Sterling, a 37-year-old black man, was shot and killed by two Baton Rouge Police Department officers in Baton Rouge, Louisiana, July 5, 2016.

SO OUT OF WORDS

In a world where too many people
have their fingers on the triggers

of guns aimed directly at black people,
we have borne witness, time

and time again, to executions
filmed on tiny cameras—

Which allow us to see too much
Which allow us to see not enough.

Judge, jury, executioner—
It's due process in the suburbs

and the city streets, on winding
country roads and highways, sidewalks

in front of the convenience store,
where the streetlights don't shine

in the back corner of a parking lot,
on the playground, behind the fence

in a field near your children's school
on the street in front of your house.

This interminable spectacle
of black death playing on a loop

over and over again until
we become numb to something

that is now a permanent part
of the American memory.

How could these grainy videos
not translate into justice?

I just don't know how to believe
change is possible

when there is so much
evidence to the contrary.

I am so out of words
in the face of such brutality.

Black lives matter, and then
in an instant, they don't.

Written and recited at the Arm in Arm (South Carolinians for Responsible Gun Ownership) rally in Marion Square, Charleston, South Carolina, following the shooting at Marjory Stoneman Douglas High School in Parkland, Florida, February 14, 2018.

AFTER EVERY MASS SHOOTING

the bullet holes are counted
and marked; casings are collected.
The coroner examines
the bodies and takes them away.
Blood is wiped clean from walls
and windows, ceiling and floors,
then yellow tape is wound
around the crime scene as if
it can contain the violence.

Soon crowds of strangers gather,
leaving flowers and teddy bears
with notes pinned to the fur
in piles at make-shift
memorials. There are vigils
with candles and song,
spontaneous circles of prayer.

After every mass shooting

the heart-shaped balloons float away
and the media trucks move
on to the next unnecessary
tragedy. No one ever sees
what an assault weapon
does to the human body.
The way a hollow point bullet

expands upon impact, shredding
every bone and organ in its path.

And no one sees the mother
returning to the empty house
and closing the heavy door
to her child's bright bedroom.
No one sees her, sitting
in the living room all night
with the lights off. No one sees
what she sees, staring into
the ragged hole, carved
into the heart of the world.

IV. ONE RIVER, ONE BOAT

"I've known rivers ancient as the world and older than the flow of human blood in human veins."

— Langston Hughes

On the occasion of Mark Sanford's inauguration as Governor of South Carolina, January 2003.

RIVERS OF WIND

Today the angels are tumbling
down through heaven's door.
All along the Coosaw
they hover in a misting halo,
until the black river
shreds into the sea. Today,
as the old oak leaves spin
into bright bunches of confetti,
oysters split open their shells
and sing. At the water's edge
lilies and tickseed bloom
white and yellow candles
for the dead. All along the Coosaw
the breaths of angels
compose the air, moving in rivers
of wind across this land.

The rivers are omnipotent.
They weave through the earth
like veins, moving for thousands
of miles. There is no beginning.
There is no end, like the moss
and trillium flowing across the forest floor,
or the ravens gathered
above the sharp edges
of the Blue Ridge Escarpment.
In the gray granite cliffs,

where they build
their winter nests of twigs and fine hair
the birds caw and chortle.
Their rumble is the sound
of a wild, free place.
From these mountain tops,
it seems you can see forever -
From the sandhills to the swampland.
From the Piedmont
to the Peedee. In all directions
today, the ever-changing colors
are splashing through the sky -

because in every heart
there is a God of hope, hiding
like a tight frightened seed,
that waits for the first smudge
of sunlight to spread
across the horizon, and later
in the purpled evening, rain.

Seeds of hope are waiting
in the sacred soil beneath our feet
and in the light and in the shadows,
spinning below the hemlocks.
Hope waits in the endless
waterfalls tumbling toward earth,
transforming into rivers
that pull us through embattled centuries.
Hope waits for the waters
to still and the currents

to empty themselves of the blood
that came before.

Hope waits for a day like today.

Hope waits for this man,
who reaches across
our divided lives.

Be still.
Be silent.

There is so much light
filling the sky here.
So much conviction
in the wind now.
Watch the seeds of hope
as they scatter far,
far across this land.

For Mark Sanford, on the occasion of his second inauguration as Governor of South Carolina, January 10, 2007.

THE WORLD IS GREEN AGAIN

"Victory, union, faith, identity, time,
The indissoluble compacts, riches, mystery
Eternal progress, the kosmos...."

— Walt Whitman, "Starting from Paumanok"

Low limbs of the live oak twist
like overlapping black rivers
across the sky. It is easy
to feel lost in the maze
of their convoluted journey,

but there are small birds
we cannot see, singing
in the silvery sun -
nests balanced on the tips
of branches like bowls of light.

An osprey looks down from a nest
of twigs and Spanish Moss.
The broad crown of the oak
is thick with green leaves rippling
in waves. Sometimes, hovering

over water, searching the surface
for fish, he remembers this tree -
the absolute permanence,
considers its great weight
and all the lives intertwining.

He exists as a mass of feathers,
talons, and bone – a dark winged
fishhawk weaving a life from air.
Loyal to this land and patient,
he trusts the hours that pass

through wind and cold bursts of rain.
Like the live oak, like this place
he inhabits with his whole heart,
he waits until the days lengthen,
and the whole world is green again.

For Nikki Randhawa Haley, on the occasion of her inauguration as Governor of South Carolina, January 12, 2011.

THE WEIGHT IT TAKES

In the white silence that is winter
return to the river, if only
for solitude. Begin at the roots.
Touch the pulse that keeps
flowing on its own. Sometimes
you will need only this.

For rivers are just a way for us
to find one another. Each rock,
the weight it takes to keep us
here; the fish, just fleeting
friendships, that will disappear
and reappear when we least expect it.

Beneath a tangle of trees,
the riverbank is an altar
holding water; the single vessel
taking in miles of spinning leaves,
lost feathers, and the dreams
of all who come here.

Now your life belongs to the world.
Hold fast to everything
beating with sunlight.
Pull us together, like water.
Be the weight that grounds us
through swirling hours of each day.
When voices shout without ceasing,
be the stillness we hear ringing in our hearts.

For Governor Nikki Haley's second inauguration, January 2015, excluded from inauguration ceremonies, subsequently read into the Congressional Record by Congressman James Clyburn, and on the South Carolina Senate floor by Senator Marlon Kimpson.

ONE RIVER, ONE BOAT

"I know there's something better down the road."
— Elizabeth Alexander

Because our history is a knot
we try to unravel, while others
try to tighten it, we tire easily
and fray the cords that bind us.

The cord is a slow-moving river,
spiraling across the land
in a succession of S's,
splintering near the sea.

Picture us all, crowded onto a boat
at the last bend in the river:
watch children stepping off the school bus,
parents late for work, grandparents

fishing for favorite memories,
teachers tapping their desks
with red pens, firemen suiting up
to save us, nurses making rounds,

baristas grinding coffee beans,
dockworkers unloading apartment size
containers of computers and toys
from factories across the sea.
Every morning a different veteran

stands at the base of the bridge
holding a cardboard sign
with misspelled words and an empty cup.

In fields at daybreak, rows of migrant
farm workers standing on ladders, break open
iced peach blossoms; their breath rising
and resting above the frozen fields like clouds.

A jonboat drifts down the river.
Inside, a small boy lies on his back;
hand laced behind his head, he watches
stars fade from the sky and dreams.

Consider the prophet John, calling us
from the edge of the wilderness to name
the harm that has been done, to make it
plain, and enter the river and rise.

It is not about asking for forgiveness.
It is not about bowing our heads in shame;
because it all begins and ends here:
while workers unearth trenches

at Gadsden's Wharf, where 100,000
Africans were imprisoned within brick walls
awaiting auction, death, or worse.
Where the dead were thrown into the water,

and the river clogged with corpses
has kept centuries of silence.
It is time to gather at the edge of the sea,
and toss wreaths into this watery grave.

And it is time to praise the judge
who cleared George Stinney's name,
seventy years after the fact,
we honor him; we pray.

Here, where the Confederate flag
flies beside the Statehouse, haunted
by our past, conflicted about the future;
at the heart of it, we are at war with ourselves

huddled together on this boat
handed down to us – stuck
at the last bend of a wide river
splintering near the sea.

In memory of Walter Scott and Muhiyidin d'Baha

A POEM FOR SOUTH CAROLINA

I TAKE THE ROLE OF POET LAUREATE SERIOUSLY; IT IS AN enormous honor and privilege. During the years I served as South Carolina's poet laureate, I have used the status of the position to accomplish many important objectives, from co-founding a literary organization to serve the writing community and the greater community, to reading handwritten poems by people who have written their entire lives and never shared their work with anyone. My goals have always been to increase literacy and literary awareness in as many ways as possible. This deeply honored position in South Carolina resulted in endless requests to speak at library openings, elementary school English classes, colleges, senior centers, lighthouse and bridge openings. I have met so many extraordinary South Carolinians, and these connections have been a deep source of joy.

While the requests are unending, and most people assume it is my duty and my expenses are covered, during the last four years attending anything has meant paying out of my own pocket. Despite my efforts on behalf of the state, during the four years Governor Nikki Haley was in office, I have received no communication from her or her staff on any matters and they cut my travel stipend. Perhaps it should have come as no surprise to hear that at Governor Haley's second inauguration there simply was no time for a poem. Three minutes is not a lot of time my friends.

At national poet laureate gatherings, we discuss the inherent difficulties of writing pieces for governors whose policies conflict with our own and the ironic fact that we often end up with better work because of that tension. Occasional poems are difficult to write; they have to work off the page and there can't be a lot of ambiguity. They also must be respectful of the occasion and not polemic. I was thinking about the piece for Governor Haley for a long time and on December 4th I posted a request on Facebook asking the question "What is your dream for SC?" I heard from more than fifty people regarding their concerns about improving our public education, embracing diversity and inclusion, and so on. One of the most extraordinary things a poem can do is to hold many disparate things together in a way that creates an entirely new meaning: one that only exists within the piece. "One River, One Boat" seems to be that kind of a poem. These disparate things are threads that run through my life but also speak deeply to others, and the response to this piece has been both moving and profound. South Carolina Congressman James E. Clyburn, who read "One River, One Boat" into the Congressional Record on the day of Governor Haley's inauguration, told me that everything he wanted to say about his seventy-six years on earth is expressed in the text. An English professor from Arizona planned to name his unborn child after me. An artist and former Howard University professor wrote that the enslaved dreamed that a writer like me would one day stand up for them and write something that holds up the mirror of truth.

These intense responses, and the media attention the work received when it was cut from Governor Haley's inauguration, have to do with forces much bigger than me. The racial unrest that began in Ferguson and spread throughout the country in late 2014, coupled with the horrific killings at the Charlie Hebdo offices in Paris in early January that united the world in defense of free speech, form the backdrop into which this piece was dropped. It was a perfect storm of circumstances, and the words resonated with many people who care deeply about social justice issues but don't necessarily have a voice. Isn't this the true job of the poet?

V. WE GRIEVE AS ONE

"…..where loss makes all things beautiful grow."

— Ross Gay

Honoring those murdered at Mother Emanuel Church, Charleston, South Carolina, June 17, 2015.

HOLY CITY

"Only love can conquer hate."
— Reverend Clementa Pinckney

Let us gather and be
silent together like stones
glittering in sunlight

so bright it hurts our eyes
emptied of tears and searching
the sky for answers.

Let us be strangers
together as we gather
in circles wherever we meet,

to stand hand in hand and sing
hymns to the heavens and pray
for the fallen and speak their names:

Clementa, Cynthia, Tywanza,
Ethel, Sharonda, Daniel,
Myra, Susie and Depayne.

They are not alone. As bells
in the spires call across
the wounded Charleston sky,

we close our eyes and listen
to the same stillness ringing
in our hearts, holding onto

one another like brothers,
like sisters because we know
wherever there is love, there is God.

Written during the dark days following June 17, 2015.

MUSIC OF DOVES ASCENDING

Yellow crime tape tied to the rod iron fence
weaves through bouquets of flowers
and wreaths made of white ribbons,
like rivers of bright pain flowing through the hours.

Weaving through bouquets of flowers,
lines of strangers bearing offerings
like rivers of bright pain flowing through the hours.
One week later; the funeral bells ring;

lines of strangers still bring offerings.
Nine doves tossed toward the sun.
One week later; the funeral bells ring,
while churches in small towns are burning.

Nine doves tossed toward the sun.
Because there are no words to sing,
while churches in small towns are burning,
a blur of white wings, ascends like music.

In memory of the first 100,000 Americans who died of Covid as of June 2020, commissioned by Circular Congregational Church, Charleston, South Carolina, June 2021.

ONE HUNDRED THOUSAND NAMES

Whether it is morning
And sunlight is seeping through
Overlapping oak branches
Bursting with bright leaves

Or late in the day, after
Rain has fallen and the scent
Of spring splashes across
The washed sky, emptied of clouds

And opening, you have arrived
At this sanctuary
Where the locked church door is
Never closed to anyone.

Step into the circle
Of grace woven from many
Threads that bind us
Across time and place.

Let us mourn together
The thousands upon thousands
Who have perished, so many
Alone, so many afraid,

So far from the people
They loved most. Perhaps you,

Or someone you know: cousin,
Co-worker, neighbor, or friend.

One hundred thousand stories
Left to tell. One hundred thousand
Voices suddenly silent.
One hundred thousand names

Etched on the altars of our hearts.
Our grief is collective, tear
Stained and bright, blue
Like a wound or the wind

Wrapping itself around you.
As you step back into the world
Where the names of the lost
are tumbling through the sky.

Christmas 2020, the first year of the global pandemic.

ADVENT

For Reverend Jeremy Rutledge

All night a steady thrum
of cold rain on the skylight.

The wind, silent and hidden
like snow falling elsewhere.

Puddles holding streetlight
shine below like earthbound stars,

as if the light came from within.
This is what we hope for.

Day breaks and we continue
waiting, which is how we live

through darkness.

In Memory of Edwin Gardner (1946-2010), community advocate for recreational spaces, killed in a bicycle accident, Charleston, South Carolina, August 2010.

THE STONES BENEATH OUR FEET

Bless the crushed flowers cradled
in bright tissue paper tied
to the white bicycle
on a street running straight
to the sea. Bless the waves paused
in the harbor and our first
shared memory of water.
Bless the travelling voices
trapped in the air as if words
were something permanent
and bigger than stones beneath
our feet. And all those small things
that carry us through the hours –
a straight line of pelicans
caught in sunlight, the ripe
orange on a blue plate, your
favorite book beside it,
jessamine winding itself
around worn windowpanes;
that sweet smell spinning through
the room until you're dizzy.
Bless each bird and turning page;
the perfect circle of rind,
piles of petals at your feet.

For Whitney and Olive

For Selma Olivia Akguel, 11-year-old Danish girl, struck and killed in Cannon Park, Charleston, South Carolina, read at the tree planting ceremony in her honor, July 2018.

NOTHING CAN CONTAIN YOU

Not wreaths woven from fresh flowers
Nor messages pinned to the stems.
Not the grief spreading across the sea
Nor this place that will mark your passing.

Because there is no understanding
of this tragedy, nor acceptance.
Because we want to celebrate
your brief beautiful life-

we wish for birds. Small and many.
Birds that come from the sea,
which isn't far. There should be one
for each year of your life.

They should descend in a rush
and smother the trees
growing here at your roadside
memorial. The feathers should be

rainbowed, dripping salt and sand
and sea foam. No fog or gray rain
for you. No storm or wind
disturbing the bright air.

And from a distance, these trees
will look like a line of crosses,
trembling beneath a sky full of song,
a sky, perpetually filling with sunlight.

On the first anniversary of my mother's death, March 18, 2016.

ALL DAY IT IS MARCH

a blur
of unspoken sadness.
Grief
is like that –

sudden
gray gust
unravelling
the hour.

My father, gone
almost five decades.
My mother
carrying on in pieces
that never
quite fit
back together.

She lived out
his life span-
exactly.
This math
is irrefutable,
like so little else
in our lives;

witnessing all
that he missed:

graduations, weddings,
grandchildren.

She even struggled
with a new husband,
which almost
became
a new life,
but never quite did.

Until one day
in March,
the month
she chose to leave.
Days bulging
with wind

singing
of loss. Days
of thaw
and confusion.

After the last cold
clear night
of the season,
pink azaleas
beginning
to bloom
along the side
of the house.
By afternoon,
she was gone.

In honor of Mother's Day, Kwame Alexander asked a dozen fellow poets for a few stanzas on how their lives—and their cooking—now mirror their mother.

I AM BECOMING MY MOTHER....

When I take handfuls of canned
Tomatoes draining in the sink
And squeeze them between my fingers
Gently, before tossing them
Into the pot simmering
With garlic and onions
On the Sunday stove—
The same way she gathered
Handfuls of my damp red curls
In a towel at bath time,
Her fingers pulsing with love
As they squeezed my hair dry,
And later, at the dinner table
When I struggled with the silverware
She reached behind me
And covered my hands in hers
Guiding me without a word
Through the maze of childhood
And the shadows beyond.

In memory of my stepfather, Robert Michael Tully, June 19, 1929 - June 5, 2011.

SUMMER DIRGE

If there is rain, let it be
lead-blue, shattering like glass
across this gray morning sky.
Let it be salt-tinged and iced
with sea. Let it sting like tears
falling, today. As we gather
at your graveside, let it rain.

The South Carolina writing community suffered an enormous loss when author Pat Conroy died in March 2016.

GREAT LOVE AND A POET'S HEART

PAT CONROY WAS ALWAYS BIGGER THAN LIFE, AND THIS quality made him seem indestructible to everyone who knew him. He was a giant of a man in all ways, and I consider myself one of the lucky ones who circled in his orbit.

It is no exaggeration to state that when we moved to Charleston in 1989 for my husband's job, the only thing I knew about this place was what I had read in Pat's novels—particularly *The Prince of Tides*. I grew up in a coastal town north of Boston, so the sea was part of my childhood. The sense of place is so palpable in Pat's work; I could smell the pluff mud rising off the pages of my paperback. I knew of Pat's love of poetry before I met him. He has a poet's heart. Attention to specific image details permeates his writing and creates a sense of place that is intoxicating. In fact, he studied with the late James Dickey and Pat was quite serious about becoming a poet.

I admire everything about Pat's writing. His sentences are dazzling and exquisitely crafted, and his language choices are exact, like a poet's. So, when I began to turn to the Lowcountry landscape for inspiration, I looked to his work to discover how to do it. I even used a line from *The Prince of Tides* as an epigraph for a pivotal poem

I wrote about all that we had lost and experienced during Hurricane Hugo: "My wound is my geography." The wound he referred to was tied to his difficult youth and his abusive father. But his themes about surviving a dysfunctional childhood gave me the confidence to write about subjects I had shied away from in my own work, like the rape of my mother as a young girl and other personal difficulties. Pat talked about how excruciating it was for him to experience the psychic pain required to write what he committed to the page, and there's a deep courage at the root of his art that I greatly admire.

It takes a certain strength to step out of your life and embrace another's, or in a larger way a group of people. And nowhere is Pat's big heart more evident than in his early years teaching on Daufuskie Island and his gorgeous book *The Water Is Wide.* This experience entered my consciousness and helped me understand that to be in this place and *not* write about the African American experience is to not really be here at all.

Our introduction, however, was not auspicious. When our mutual friend Dottie Frank introduced me to Pat, she said, "This is my poet friend Marjory I told you about, the one whose cousin hit Stephen King with a car." (This cousin was a distant one, connected to me through the marriage of one of my mother's many sisters.) Pat, of course, was a friend of Stephen King's, and yet he was still nice to me.

Pat and Cassandra have been kind and supportive at every stage of my writing life here. I am so grateful. They served on the Advisory Board of LILA (Lowountry Initiative for the Literary Arts), an organization I co-founded. They were always generous and donated signed books whenever requested. If I was in Beaufort doing a reading or event, one or both of them was invariably there. Pat, of course, was a self-proclaimed blurb slut! And he would never write anything negative about another writer. His generous spirit set a tone that trickled down the writing ranks. If the greatest among us can give endorsements, then each of us can do the same. His approach to such things reminded everyone to be supportive of one another.

Pat didn't send me many emails, but when he did, they mattered so much. I always got such a kick out of his email address: atticus@.... His notes were always about my writing or some literary accomplishment and were filled with over-the-top comments that brought tears to my eyes: "I read your new edition of collected poems yesterday and the Lowcountry can thank the gods that your life brought you to Charleston." When I was inducted into the South Carolina Academy of Authors, he sent a note describing how much it meant to him when he was selected, since he was a military brat and could never quite say where home was. He reminded me that I was "an immigrant from New England" and suggested "let them carve that on your tombstone, girl." He referred to me as "his" poet laureate, which of course meant the world to me. He believed in me and supported me as a writer, and it meant more to me than I can say. Pat signed his emails "Great Love" and that is what he brought to this place, his writing, his friends, and family, and the world. Great Love.

I loved his sense of humor; he had nicknames for everyone. Dottie Frank was the *Dotted One*, his wife Cassandra was the *Dragon Lady*, his friend John Warley was *Lord John.* But, no one brought out Pat's zany sense of humor more than his friend Bernie Schein. They were like a *Saturday Night Live* skit. Years after the movie *The Prince of Tides* was filmed here, I heard the infamous stories about Bernie calling Pat whenever a book came out and imitating a famous movie star or director, like Robert Redford, who expressed a desire to make the book into a film. So, when Barbara Streisand actually did phone Pat to see about optioning the book, he thought it was Bernie and hung up the phone. I can still remember the great South Carolina

Film Commissioner Isabelle Hill standing in our kitchen asking us if we knew anything about Pat Conroy. *What was his problem? Why wouldn't he answer Barbara Streisand's phone calls?* Little did I know....

I regret that I never got to properly say good-bye to Pat and tell him how much he meant to me, but I think he knew. I know how hard he fought to stay alive. I know he was still working on a manuscript. I know that Cassandra never left his side, and that he was surrounded by the great love of family and friends.

My mother entered hospice care on March 2, 2016, and she passed away soon after that. I will always associate these two losses in my life. Pat died on March 4, but that week in the midst of Pat's funeral and all the arrangements Bernie's dear daughter Maggie Schein called and texted and checked in on me. Pat's brother Tim sent me text messages with a line from a favorite poem almost every day, and Cassandra sent us a box of fruit. In the throes of their grief, those closest to Pat, sent their love to me and my family. Every day I felt that big Conroy heart was still beating in the world. It always will be.

In memory of Muhiyidin d'Bhaha, Charleston-based Black Lives Matter Activist, murdered in New Orleans in February 2018. This poem was read at his funeral.

REWRITING THE WORLD WITHOUT YOU

One bird
calling
through winter
dawn repeats

like a bell
unwinding
the night
sky still
crowded
with overlapping clouds

the sun
behind
is silent

the sound
of the world without
your drum now

only the wind
is singing

VI. HERE IS WHERE WE EAT THE SUN

"Every morning the world is created.
Under the orange sticks of the sun..."

— **Mary Oliver**

For the celebration of the painting Seeking, by Jonathan Green, Charleston, South Carolina, 2008 (Jonathan Green Week).

SEEKING

It happens in stillness. Because it is night
you hear snakes drop from the oak
and other things you cannot name
passing beneath or above you. Trees
so thick the stars are mute.
Close your eyes. The immensity
of such unquantifiable light
fills the emptiness that once was
memory. After the hunger
and solitude, dreams, and the dead
speaking as if they are with you,
it happens when the oak begins to burn
from within. And you welcome the flames.

On the occasion of the solar eclipse, August 21, 2017.

ACROSS THE SILENCE

Astronomy flourished at the dawn of civilization;
between the Tigris and Euphrates, Babylonian
astronomers watched the skies closely.
We have the records. When heavenly signs appeared, the ancients were
both fascinated and terrified.
Watching a celestial dragon devour the sun,
the Chinese foretold the future of the Emperor,
banging pots and drums to scare the creature from the sky.
Although many believed in bad omens, The Prophet Mohammed
described cosmic spectacles as a demonstration of Allah's might.
While ancient Greeks accurately measured angles
of shadows cast at noon on the summer solstice,
estimating the earth's circumference, Archilochus,
the poet soldier, wrote that nothing is beyond hope,
and anything is possible while the light of the shining sun
hides at mid-day and the world plunges into darkness.
What will we believe, when we stop our days
to watch the barely perceptible dent in the sun, widen
into an arc, casting a stripe of shadow across the earth?
As the fiery ring of the corona shimmers in darkness
and the stars and planets appear across the silence
that must be endless, we would be wise to bang pots
to keep the dragons away and chant the Greek meaning
for the awe-inspiring event, *abandonment, abandonment.*

For my husband Peter, on our 40th wedding anniversary, June 27, 2021.

RIVER SONG

Our house is a river
flowing by gardens of fruit
and lavender butterfly
bushes, magnolia and fig
trees tangled in vines that swirl
beneath moonlight and star shine.

Mountain born, granite fed
river of feathers and glass,
where light gathers each morning
and evening as birdsong braids
the air into one green song
humming like a heartbeat.

Passed astonished snow swept
islands and the city
rising at the edge of the sea,
the river rushes in a fury
under the great steel buildings
glowing like ripe volcanoes

in the blue-black night. City
of music and light, crisscrossed
with train tracks and avenues
bearing multitudes. City of smoke.
City of dreams collecting
like seeds and scattered on water.

Our house is a river
where books have gathered
in great piles along the banks
before the flood and after,
dog leafed, molded and torn,
tear stained and treasured.

We crossed a bridge and returned
wounded and singing, carrying
butterflies and lightning
in our pockets, children
strapped to our backs, water
rushing beneath us
like an unwritten story.

For my son Taylor on his 21st birthday.

WATERBOY

Waterboy sprung from the sea,
return whenever you feel
a longing for something
luminous you cannot name.
When turtles swim through your sleep
follow them into the deep,
though it is dark and difficult
diving into those places
of multiplying silence.

Because your home was built
on a narrow mound of sand
held down by wandering vines,
where turtles dig deep holes
into the dunes for nests,
the eggs they will abandon
with blind hope and the kind
of faith we all hunger for,
return with flipper and wing,
scales that sparkle near the sun-
lit surface of the sea, to float
beneath a blur of clouds,
letting black sand spill slowly
from your opening hands.

For the graduates of the Art Institute of Charleston, June 2011.

A PLACE FOR YOU

Take time to hover at the still
mouth of this ancient harbor
then rise into the air, which holds

a place for you. Let the wind
off the sea lift you up and hold
you above the daily cacophony,

before your hours fill
with unintentional clutter,
the way small clouds seem

to occupy the sky on days
you are not paying attention.
Do not ignore the ordinary -

each drop of gray drizzle,
every stone and snapped twig,
all the creatures, thriving here.

Because there are questions
with no answers and many days
you will wish to forget,

savor each hour of sunlight
when it permeates the sky,
streaming through you

like music. Listen to the glittering
wings beating within
the engine of your heart.

For Jean Hoefer Toal, First Woman Chief Justice of the South Carolina Supreme Court, at the unveiling of her portrait Columbia Museum of Art, May 2015.

SOARING

In the garden, after hours of rain,
at sunrise, red petals begin
poking slowly through
the swaddling of green sepals.

A woman sees tulips
waken beside her as she walks.
Happiness spreads within
her heart. There is a nest

in the oak tree. Each morning
she pauses, as if the beige eggs
were hers. She feels responsible
for anything that delicate

and vulnerable. She knows
there will be one,
whose featherless head
will emerge before the others.

The one whose wings will be first
to lift into the sun-drenched air.
The one who will always be
soaring above the rest of us.

For John C. Miller on his retirement as CEO of Denny's, Spartanburg, South Carolina, July 2022.

PRAISE FOR THE JOURNEY

"Wherever you stand, Be the soul of that place."
— Rumi

A swirl of butterflies brightens
the steep path you have carved
through the undergrowth.
Clearing away the tangle of trees
and thick vines, you lifted
each stone blocking the way,
filling the cracks
that others made before you
fixing every broken thing
no matter how small,
finding joy on the journey
and sharing it.

Guided by a light
from within, you always found
something unexpected,
like feathers falling
slowly from a gray sky,
or leaves, still glistening
with rain. Green sounds
spilling around you
as you climbed, step by step
guiding others, offering
a hand without being asked,

showing the way forward
by quiet example.

Consider the live oaks
tilting toward one another
across the path,
limbs intertwining
into one body overhead
like a new creation,
the world beneath
unfolding in the light
you have made
for all of us.

For the opening of the Charleston Wine & Food Festival, March 2015.

HERE IS WHERE WE EAT THE SUN

It is not about Sweat Tea and magnolias,
although a little sugar never hurt anyone-
and there is nothing better than shrimp and grits
for breakfast, a supper of Hopping John,
collards, butter beans and corn bread.

It's more the ease and abundance that delights—
the way the earth, gives back each day
in tangles of wild asparagus or rice,
blackberries growing along the edges of a backyard.

And gardens where marbleized green globes
of watermelon spin against the dark earth,
beside tomatoes tied to sticks and herbs
flourishing in the corner: sage, oregano
and thyme; mint filling the morning air.

It's the wonder of squash vines, filling with sun-
light exploding in rows of yellow blossoms,
the way fingers of lime green cucumbers
poke through curled leaves like offerings.

It's long summer evenings on the back porch,
boiled peanut shells tossed in a bowl,
picking at blue crabs dragged on a string
from the Atlantic that morning…

Maybe it's the way peaches pull their color
from the sky bursting over the sea

or how oysters, still covered in pluff mud,
sitting in the world of their shells,
taste exactly like the beginning of time.

In recognition of the Charleston Symphony Orchestra League's Sumer Fête, June 27, 2021.

SPIN A SONG: RUMI

Walk out of your room
beneath the morning sky;
let the sun enter your heart,

and find a way
to keep it there.

Make a song from the light
falling through the air;
and dance even when
you are alone.

Dance if you are still sad.
Dance when you are tired.
Dance until your feet lift
off the ground like wings.

And later, when the stars
are spinning in the night,
put your ear to the ground
and listen to the songs
rising up from the earth

everywhere you go.
There is music.

NOTES AND ACKNOWLEDGMENTS

I. REIMAGINING HISTORY

Epigraph (page 3)
From "Native Guard" *January 1863*, *Native Guard* By Natasha Tretheway, New York: Houghton Mifflin, 2006.

"1937"
Inspired by the exhibition *The Bitter Years: Dorthea Lange and Walter Evans Photography from the Martin Z Marguiles/ Sharecropper wife and mother of seven children, Near Chesnee, South Carolina* photographer Dorthea Lange.

II. DESPITE GRAVITY

Epigraph (page 25)
From *The Prince of Tides* By Pat Conroy, New York: Houghton Mifflin, 1986.

III. HOW TO LOVE THIS WORLD

Epigraph (page 43)
From "Dedication," in *Selected Poems* by Czeslaw Milosz, New York: The Ecco Press, 1973.

"Militants Ban School Bells in a town in Somalia" is inspired by *The New York Times* article by Mohamed Ibrahim, "Militants Ban School Bells in a town in Somalia" April 15, 2010.

"So Out of Words" is inspired by Roxanne Gay's editorial "When Black Lives Stop Mattering," *The New York Times*, July 16, 2016.

IV. ONE RIVER, ONE BOAT

Epigraph (page 59)
From "The Negro Speaks of Rivers" in *Selected Poems of Langston Hughes* by Langston Hughes, New York: Vintage Books, 1990.

The line "Now your life belongs to the world" in "The Weight it Takes," refers to "The Strength of Fields" By James Dickey, | Poetry Foundation

V. WE GRIEVE AS ONE

Epigraph (page 73)
From "feet," in *Catalog of Unabashed Gratitude* by Ross Gay, Pittsburgh: University of Pittsburgh Press, 2015.

VI. HERE IS WHERE WE EAT THE SUN

Epigraph (page 93)
From "Morning Poem," in *Dream Work* by Mary Oliver, New York: Atlantic Monthly Press, 1986.

BACK COVER

Quote (Congressman James E. Clyburn, 6th District of SC)
Vol. 161 No. 7 Wednesday, January 14, 2015 Congressional Record, Tribute to the South Carolina Poet Laureate, Marjory Wentworth by The Honorable James E. Clyburn

ACKNOWLEDGMENTS

Grateful acknowledgement is made to the editors of the following publications in which these poems and essays first appeared. Some updates have been made for clarity. Special thanks to The Black Earth Institute for its generous support.

ESSAYS

"A Most Unexpected Muse," from *State of the Heart, South Carolina Writer on the Places They Love,* edited by Aïda Rogers, Published by USC Press, 2013.

"A Poem for South Carolina" Foreword *South Carolina Writers on the Places They Love*, Volume 2, Edited by Aïda Rogers, The University of South Carolina Press, 2015.

"Great Love and a Poet's Heart" *Our Prince of Scribes: Writers Remember Pat Conroy,* Edited by Nicole Seitz and Jonathan Haupt, The University of Georgia Press, 2018.

POEMS

"The Architecture of Containment," "1937," "Flight," and "Nothing is Abandoned", *Jasper Project Online,* Al Black's Poetry of the People with Marjory Wentworth, April 20, 2024.

"I am becoming my mother" "Twelve Poets Created This Ode to Mothers—and Their Kitchens," edited By Kwame Alexander, *Bon Appetit,* May 7, 2021.

"In the Shadows of Nuremberg," "One Hundred Thousand Names," "Requiem for Rice." *About Place Journal, Works of Resistance, Resilience,* Volume VI, Issue II, October 2020.

"In the Shadows of Nuremberg." *American Society of International Law,* 2017.

"So Out of Words." *Sojourners,* June 2017.

"Spin a Song: Rumi" *Out of Wonder, Poems Celebrating Poets* by Kwame Alexander with Chris Colderley and Marjory Wentworth, 2017, Candlewick Press.

"Holy City," "One River, One Boat," and "Music of Doves Ascending." *Illuminations,* 31, Summer 2016.

"Holy City" *The Post and Courier* newspaper pull-out commemorative issue (6/21/2015)

"Washington Square, Charleston Tent City after the Earthquake." *Found Anew, Poetry and Prose Inspired by the South Carolinian Library Digital Collections,* edited by R. Mac Jones and Ray McManus, University of South Carolina Press, 2015.

"One River, One Boat." NPR, Jan. 14, 2015, coladaily.com, *The Post and Courier,* Al Jeezera, and numerous other mentions in national media when Congressman Jim Clyburn read the poem into Congressional Record on Jan. 14, 2015.

"River Song" *Southern Women's Review, Volume 7,* 2014.

"Militants Ban School Bells in a Town in Somalia." *Fall Lines,* 2014.

"Waterboy." *Prairie Schooner*, Volume 87: Number 2, Summer 2013.

"Seeking." *Seeking: Poetry and Prose Inspired by the Art of Jonathan Green,* 2013, University of South Carolina Press, (co-edited with Kwame Dawes).

"A Place for You," "The Stones Beneath Our Feet," *Fledgling Rag,* Issue 10, 2011.

"The Weight It Takes," *Connotation Press: An Online Artifact,* 2011

"Charleston Rooftops," *The Dead Mule,* April 2009.

The following poems were published in *New and Selected, Poems* by Marjory Wentworth, The University of South Carolina Press, 2014: "Carolina Umbra," "Hurricane Season," "River," "Tangled," "Sand," "Despite Gravity," "Seeking," "Charleston Rooftops," "A Place for You," "The Weight it Takes," "The Stones Beneath Our Feet."

www.ingramcontent.com/pod-product-compliance
Lightning Source LLC
LaVergne TN
LVHW051010080826
845145LV00009B/2544

9781929647996